D1561324

IN A CLASS OF HER OWN

Written by

KATHLEEN GOULD LUNDY

Illustrated by

JEFF ALWARD

RUBY BRIDGES

LUCILLE BRIDGES

ABON BRIDGES

MRS. HENRY

REAL PEOPLE IN HISTORY

RUBY BRIDGES: The first African American child to attend an all-white school in New Orleans, Louisiana.

LUCILLE BRIDGES: Ruby's mother — a courageous woman who insisted that her daughter should have the same education as a white child.

ABON BRIDGES: Ruby's father — a gentle man who feared for his daughter's safety and well-being.

MRS. HENRY: The schoolteacher who taught Ruby in her first year at William Frantz Public School in New Orleans.

Contents

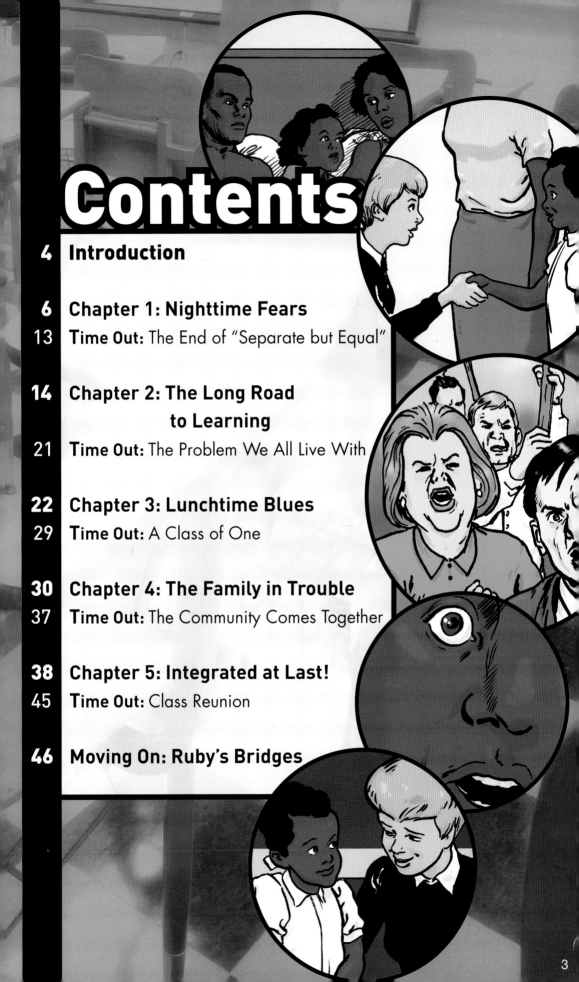

I n the 1950s, African Americans in the U.S. began to press for civil rights — that is, to be given the same treatment as other citizens of the nation. They were led by Dr. Martin Luther King Jr. and they demanded an end to unfair treatment.

African Americans were treated especially unfairly in the South. During the American Civil War (1861–1865), the southern states had fought for the right to keep owning black people as slaves.

The South lost the war and slavery was abolished. Yet a century later, black people were still kept separate from white people in various ways. This was called segregation. Blacks were not allowed in many restaurants. They had to sit in the backs of buses, behind white people. Black children went to different schools from white children.

TIMELINE

1954 »	1955 »	1957 »	1958 »
Ruby Bridges is born. The U.S. Supreme Court rules that schools must be integrated.	Rosa Parks is arrested in Alabama for refusing to give her seat on a bus to a white person.	President Eisenhower orders federal troops to escort nine African American students to a white school in Little Rock, Arkansas.	The Bridges family moves from Mississippi to New Orleans, Louisiana.

In 1954, the U.S. Supreme Court ruled that schools had to be "integrated." Children of all races had to be educated together. Many schools in the South ignored this ruling.

In 1960, six-year-old Ruby Bridges became the first African American child to attend an all-white school in New Orleans, Louisiana. This is her story.

Note: In the U.S. today, black people of African origin are generally referred to as African Americans.

WHAT'S THE STORY?

This story is set in an actual time in history and depicts real people.

1960 »	1964 »	1968 »	1996 »
New Orleans schools are told they must be integrated. Ruby attends first grade at an all-white school.	Dr. Martin Luther King Jr. wins the Nobel Peace Prize for his leadership of the civil rights movement.	Dr. Martin Luther King Jr. is assassinated in Memphis, Tennessee.	Ruby Bridges is reunited with her first grade teacher on a television show.

Chapter 1: Nighttime Fears

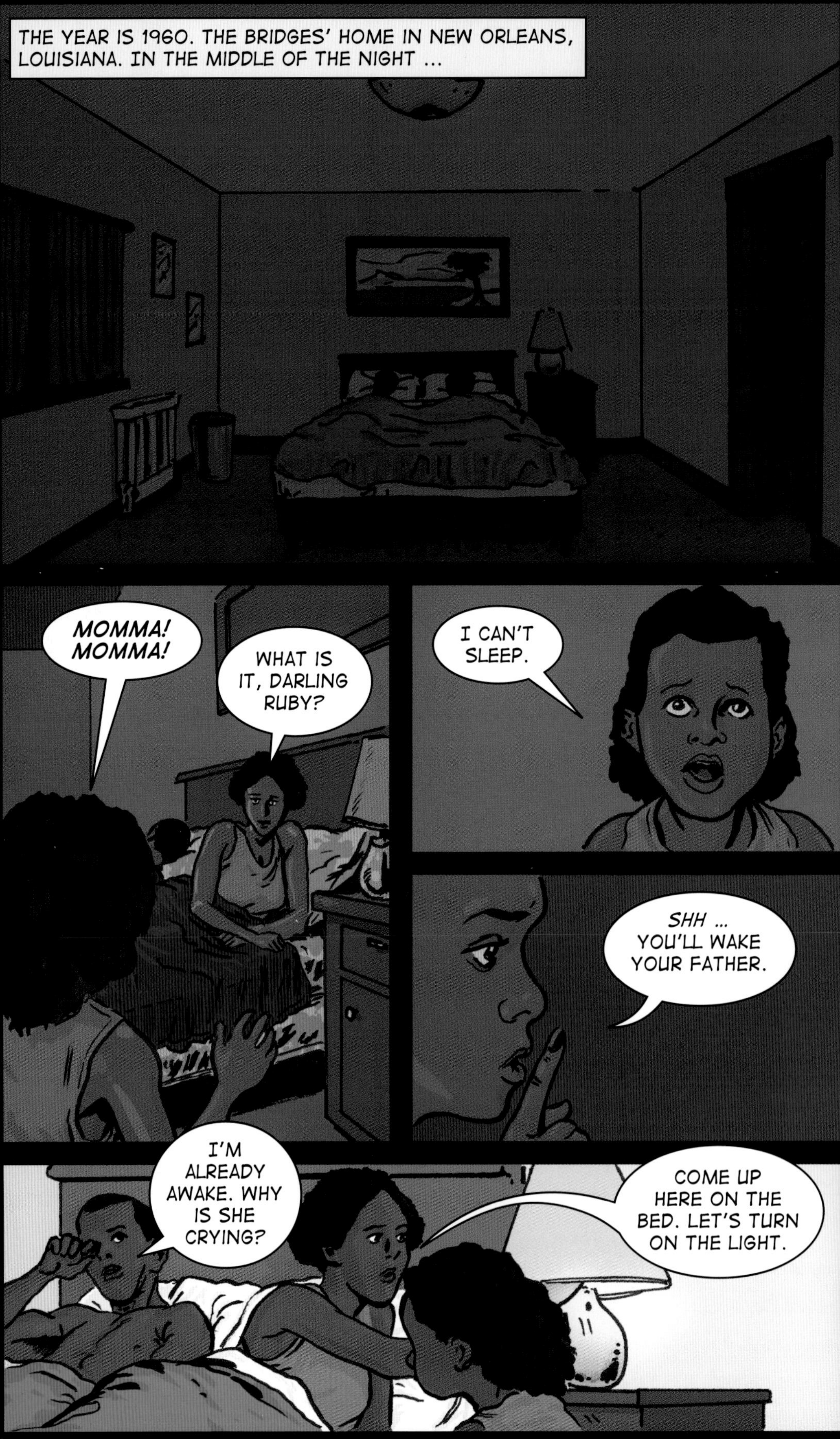

BUT WHY DOES IT HAVE TO BE OUR CHILD WHO CHANGES THE COURSE OF HISTORY? WHY HER? WHY US?

WHY? WHY? YOU KNOW WHY!

YOU AND I AND MILLIONS OF OUR PEOPLE ARE TIRED OF LIVING AS SECOND-CLASS CITIZENS IN OUR OWN COUNTRY!

"DRINKING FROM WATER FOUNTAINS THAT ARE FOR COLORED MEN AND WOMEN ...

HAVING TO SIT AT THE BACK OF BUSES BECAUSE WE'RE NOT WHITE ..."

WHY SHOULD OUR CHILDREN GET A SECOND-CLASS EDUCATION BECAUSE OF THE COLOR OF THEIR SKIN?

Ruby and U.S. Marshals

THE END OF "SEPARATE BUT EQUAL"

Before 1954, there were different schools for white and African American children in the United States. Although the practice was known as "separate but equal" education, white schools usually had better facilities than black schools.

In 1954, the U.S. Supreme Court ruled against "separate but equal" education. However, many schools in the southern states — including Louisiana — chose to ignore this ruling. They continued to take only white students.

LOUISIANA

New Orleans

In 1960, a federal court gave Louisiana a deadline for school integration. The New Orleans school board began to test African American children to find out who could be admitted to its white schools.

Six children passed this test. One of them, Ruby Bridges, chose to go to William Frantz Public School, an all-white elementary school in her neighborhood.

RUBY, GO HOME!

SUDDENLY ...

SPLAT!

COME ON, RUBY. TIME TO STEP OUT OF THE CAR.

THE PROBLEM WE ALL LIVE WITH

Although she lived only a few blocks from the William Frantz Public School, Ruby had to be escorted to school by federal marshals. This was because crowds of angry people had gathered to protest her presence in an all-white school. These people wanted segregation to continue.

The crowds shouted and threw things at Ruby. Years later, one of the marshals recalled: "For a little girl six years old going into a strange school with four strange deputy marshals … she showed a lot of courage. She never cried. She didn't whimper. She just marched along like a little soldier. And we're all very proud of her."

In 1964, the famous American artist Norman Rockwell made a painting of Ruby walking to school with the marshals. He called it *The Problem We All Live With*.

The Problem We All Live With
by Norman Rockwell

DURING THE LUNCH HOUR ...

I'M HUNGRY, BUT ...

...I'M AFRAID

RUBY HIDES HER SANDWICH ...

... AND HER MILK.

RUBY DOES VERY WELL AT HER LESSONS. SHE ENJOYS LEARNING FROM MRS. HENRY.

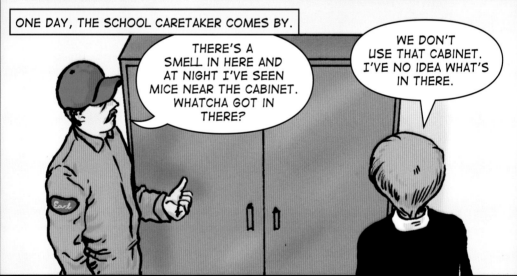

ONE DAY, THE SCHOOL CARETAKER COMES BY.

THERE'S A SMELL IN HERE AND AT NIGHT I'VE SEEN MICE NEAR THE CABINET. WHATCHA GOT IN THERE?

WE DON'T USE THAT CABINET. I'VE NO IDEA WHAT'S IN THERE.

WELL, I SUGGEST WE TAKE A LOOK.

TIME OUT!

A Class of One

Ruby spent her first year of school as the only student in Mrs. Henry's class. Most of the other students had been taken out of the school by their parents. A few white families supported integration, but it was difficult for their children to go to school while angry crowds protested outside. These white families were threatened by others who wanted segregation.

Ruby made news headlines across the nation. There were riots in New Orleans. White people drove through black neighborhoods at night leaving burning crosses behind them. Whites and blacks were angry with one another.

The mayor of New Orleans appealed for calm. The New Orleans school board asked the federal court to overturn the integration bill. They failed, and the school had to remain open for Ruby.

ONE MORNING AT BREAKFAST ...

WHERE'S POPPA? WHY ISN'T HE GETTING UP FOR BREAKFAST?

YOUR POPPA IS SLEEPING IN TODAY.

IS HE FEELING POORLY?

HE'LL BE ALL RIGHT. NOTHING TO WORRY ABOUT. IT'S TIME YOU GET READY FOR SCHOOL.

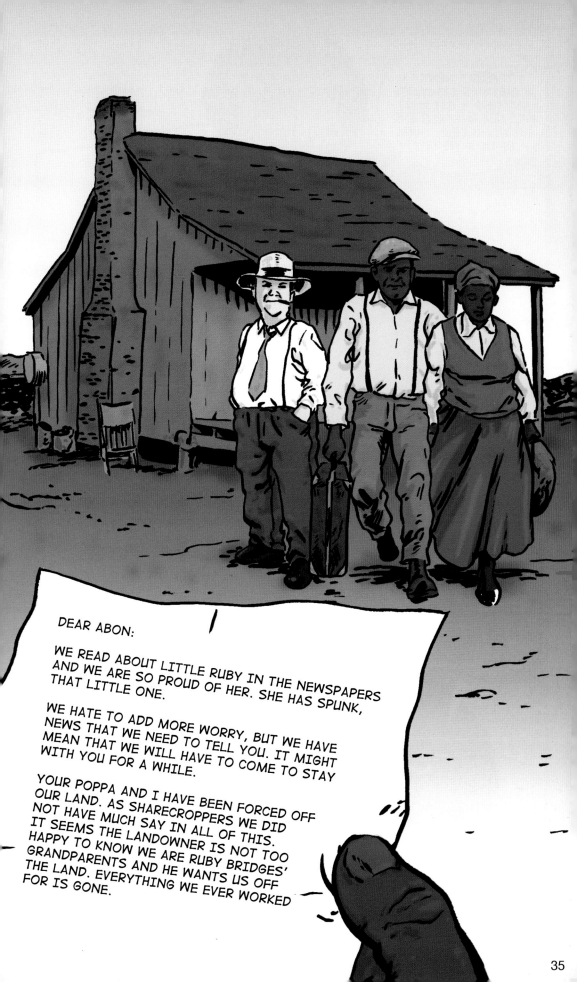

DEAR ABON:

WE READ ABOUT LITTLE RUBY IN THE NEWSPAPERS AND WE ARE SO PROUD OF HER. SHE HAS SPUNK, THAT LITTLE ONE.

WE HATE TO ADD MORE WORRY, BUT WE HAVE NEWS THAT WE NEED TO TELL YOU. IT MIGHT MEAN THAT WE WILL HAVE TO COME TO STAY WITH YOU FOR A WHILE.

YOUR POPPA AND I HAVE BEEN FORCED OFF OUR LAND. AS SHARECROPPERS WE DID NOT HAVE MUCH SAY IN ALL OF THIS. IT SEEMS THE LANDOWNER IS NOT TOO HAPPY TO KNOW WE ARE RUBY BRIDGES' GRANDPARENTS AND HE WANTS US OFF THE LAND. EVERYTHING WE EVER WORKED FOR IS GONE.

THE COMMUNITY COMES TOGETHER

Ruby's grandparents had been sharecroppers in Mississippi for 25 years. As sharecroppers, they grew crops on land rented from a landlord. When the landlord found out they were Ruby's grandparents, he told them to leave.

Ruby's father also lost his job because of the integration issue. One day, the white owners of the corner store refused to sell food to the Bridges family.

The Bridges family had friends who supported them through this period. Ruby recalls that friends of her parents would come over to help her get ready for school. Some of them would walk behind the federal marshals' car that drove her to school. People from all over the country sent letters of support. They even made donations to help her family through this time.

BACK IN THE CLASSROOM ...

I'M SO SORRY THE PRINCIPAL IS GOING TO CHANGE YOUR GRADES.

THAT'S ALL RIGHT, MRS. HENRY. THE PRINCIPAL CANNOT CHANGE WHAT IS IN MY HEAD AND MY HEART.

YOU'RE REMARKABLE, RUBY. I'LL NEVER FORGET YOU.

THE NEXT YEAR, RUBY GOES TO SECOND GRADE. THE PROTESTERS ARE GONE.

IN THE NEW CLASSROOM, SHE SEES CHILDREN OF DIFFERENT RACES.

THE SCHOOL HAS BEEN INTEGRATED AT LAST.

CLASS REUNION

TIME OUT!

Ruby never missed a day of school in her first grade class. Ruby and Mrs. Henry, her teacher, became very close during the year they spent together. Mrs. Henry was originally from Boston. During the year at New Orleans, she had to endure other white people's anger because she taught Ruby Bridges. She and her husband found it very difficult to make friends in New Orleans because of this. After that year, Mrs. Henry returned to Boston. She and Ruby did not see each other again for 35 years.

Ruby continued with her education and graduated from an integrated high school. She went to business school and became a travel agent. She married and had four sons.

Dr. Robert Coles, a psychiatrist, was very concerned about Ruby's ordeal. He volunteered to help her. Years later, he wrote a book about her called *The Story of Ruby Bridges*. It was through this book that Mrs. Henry came to be reunited with Ruby in 1996 on *The Oprah Winfrey Show*.

Ruby reunited with Mrs. Henry

MOVING ON

RUBY'S BRIDGES

In 1993, Ruby's youngest brother was killed in a shooting, leaving behind four daughters. Ruby raised her nieces together with her four sons. Her nieces happened to be students at William Frantz Public School. When Ruby took them to school every morning, she felt like she was walking into her past.

Ruby volunteered at her old school, working as a bridge between parents and the school's staff. When she heard about Dr. Coles's book, she decided to continue the work of integration that she had begun as a six-year-old child.

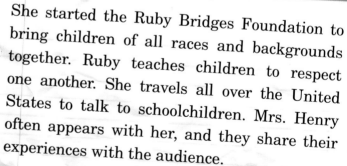

She started the Ruby Bridges Foundation to bring children of all races and backgrounds together. Ruby teaches children to respect one another. She travels all over the United States to talk to schoolchildren. Mrs. Henry often appears with her, and they share their experiences with the audience.

Ruby continues to fight for civil rights, including the right of everyone to live in society without fear of unfair treatment.

Ruby reads to schoolchildren

"EACH AND EVERY ONE OF US IS BORN WITH A CLEAN HEART. OUR BABIES KNOW NOTHING ABOUT HATE OR RACISM ..."

RUBY BRIDGES

INDEX